The daring directness of Heloise de Sat   drink,
sex and yoga, with hope and violation   e's an
exciting new poet who fuses social me   namic
and memorable poetry.
— Daljit Nagra

Rein It In is immediately and intensely readable, but reveals its depth gradually throughout the sequence. Whether in indignities coolly observed or tentative steps towards trust, de Satge captures the subtext of what's said and unsaid, the chaos of being 'a magnet for everything good and bad', but always with the joy and the risk of being fully alive to the world, the sheer value of a moment you wish would last. There are delightful inflections of the New York School and the British Poetry Revival, but this is a poet who can wear influences lightly, creating something new, resilient, personal and resonant.
— Luke Kennard

Rein It In examines girlhood experiences many of us will recognise. The way we hold our keys in our hand, the sting of awkward sex, the joy of the 'hot girl walk'. But all the while, this pamphlet invites us to question what 'girlhood' actually means.

Are the more excruciating rites of passage - the unwanted advances of men in dodgy Wetherspoons, the expensive turmeric detoxes, the lack of orgasms something we must endure? Or can we write ourselves into a different reality?

Rein It In is a confident debut that throws up big questions by exploring the intimate, I thoroughly enjoyed it.
— Talia Randall

Prepare for a world where speech has its own rules. Sentences take their own tuns, thoughts follow new structures and phrases become their own idioms. What we get is a joyful yet sincere rush of conversation, entwined with a rare personability that makes it feel like the poet is speaking directly to you, over a table of pints in Spoons. On display here is a bold honouring of moments, made all the more powerful by de Satgé's skill in blending everyday speech with loaded soundbites. The result is something strikingly relatable. A voice not to be reined in.
— Jasmine Gardosi

REIN IT IN

Héloïse de Satgé is a poet and facilitator from London. She completed both her undergraduate and postgraduate degrees at the University of Birmingham. She runs both a regular poetry night and co-runs a monthly poetry workshop. She also provides poetry mentoring. This is her first poetry pamphlet.

ISBN: 978-1-916938-22-9

Cover designed by Aaron Kent

Edited and Typeset by Aaron Kent

Broken Sleep Books Ltd
PO BOX 102
Llandysul
SA44 9BG

CONTENTS

Rein It In

Héloïse de Satgé

Broken Sleep Books

.

I posted a picture with you
from our trip to Madrid.
My mum said *oh ells,*
you look plastered.
I thought I just looked
in love.

Wanting

THE GIRLS

This is for the ugly girls, the bloated girls, the girls who vape, the girls who have vaped so many watermelon lost marys on nights out that now watermelon makes them nauseous, the girls who pay for their drinks, the girls who refuse to pay for their drinks, the girls who delete then immediately redownload tinder, the girls who aren't sure if they are girls, the girls who are questioning, the citalopram girls, the sertraline girls, the girls who love girls, the girls who cut their hair, the girls who are on OnlyFans, the girls who are making *bank*, the girls who cards have been declined for Tesco Meal deals, the girls who love being girls but sometimes hate what it means, the girls who get called "girls" by men at work, the girls who give away pads and tampons as freely as compliments, the girls who pretend to know other girls when they see danger, the girls who grit their teeth, the girls who grip their keys, the girls who have ever felt uncomfortable, the girls who are trying, the girls who are trying even though they don't want to, the girls who give up, the girls who are here, the girls who are here reading this right now, I love you, I love you specifically, I love girls, I love you so much.

I'd known since we were in primary school.

get the drinks in.

"hot girl summer".   lost a lot of weight   broken up with

free drinks

kissing   A-levels

empty   .

Spoons

fucked,   pint

shot.   holding my

I would never get with this man sober.

embarrassed.

tory.   throwing up   1am,

Brixton Road.   embarrassed

this boy knows me really well

GET THE FUCK UP, GET A FUCKING GRIP BITCH, I WILL LEAVE
YOU HERE IN 10, 9, 8

1am,   Brixton Road.

relieved, and drunk,

haven't seen

him since   go

back to his.

I can't get home fast enough.   "did

you kiss him though?"

CONKER 1

Esther used to collect conkers,
filling up her too-big grey blazer pockets until they hung down low,
brown pebbles knick knocking against the sides of her knees.

I used to make fun of her for it.
I felt too old for school,
not to be confused with "too cool", (I was not cool),
too old,
too grown, after too many
hands up skirts and
being followed home.

Maybe the conkers weren't childish at all,
less a random collection and more
nature made bullets to cut through mud-slick boys.

.

I have opened a bottle of Aldi red wine and the texts I sent you in 2016 have poured out,
like I might as well have opened a bottle of Smirnoff ice,
these messages are seeping in nostalgic cringe, all "LOL" and "long time no speak,"
I'm wincing at how I used to beg it with you, like

> *omg did you see how callum got with ellie at emily's 18th ?*
> and
> *reply to me pls*
> and
> *hey, text me*
> *your mate touched me last night*
> *who are you chirpsing?*
> *your mate touched me last night*
> *are you going to Joe's?*
> *your mate touched me last night*
> *did your brother get us any booze?*

your mate touched me last night and I didn't want him to

your mate touched me last night and I told him to stop but he kept going please don't
cause a fuss I don't know if this counts as cheating I don't think it does I was so drunk
he kept pouring larger and larger shots and told me he's always fancied me always
looked at me across the English lit classroom and I swear, my eyes rolled so far back
and then went my neck I could not keep my head up and even now it all aches from
lolling into a comma, which maybe encouraged him to keep going but I swear I wanted
him to stop

It's almost a shame I never sent any of these texts,
that they only poured out of the bottle in the present tense.
I could tell you about how much has changed since then,
like how I no longer drink Smirnoff ice,
I'm so grown now, so past it,
armed with Aldi's finest I don't let boys get away with touching me,
mate or not,
drunk or not,
18 or 25 or 50 or
I could just leave it,

brush it under shrugs,
and before I know it my wine is done,
and this sofa has never been more comfy, has never been more forgiving,
has never supported my head as well as this,
in this drunk, sweet bliss

I WANT TO GET TO KNOW YOU,

to kiss the tip
of your ambitions over the course
of an evening, then move to
tongues, toying
your words in my wine-
infused mouth and swallow
your gossip – this will tip
me over into immense
climax.

DANIEL

I am reading you my poems and you are listening.
You're going to forget everything by tomorrow,
but still, you are listening,
up until I move from whimsical quips to
MY EX DID THIS

I am reading you my poems and you are listening,
up until you want to kiss me instead,
boundaries elbowed out the window and I am
singing to your lips instead about being a
poor wayfaring stranger or just
drunk and ironically a magnet for
everything, good and bad, but
it's alright.
It's alright.
It's alright.

.

I feel uncomfortable
I feel uncomfortable
I feel uncomfortable
My stomach is full
My stomach is so full
My stomach is too full
How can a stomach be this full
It's not possible for a stomach to be this full

Does this mean
Does this mean
Does this mean

HOT CHOCOLATES AT THE INN

There is a tattoo parlour next to a funeral home across the street from the inn where they have two kinds of dairy alternative milks.

We have to leave soon, you tell me,
as we're slightly far from home and you have plans in a couple of hours.

I think, that's fair enough,
but I'm yet to write a poem with a clever quip
on the significance of a tattoo parlour
being next to a funeral home –
how they are both places of permanence and irreversible events
and both contain the potential for flowers and
negative responses from close relatives.

It's probably best that I don't have the time to spell all this out,
but I want to stay for a little longer anyway,
not necessarily because the hot chocolate is good
or because my feet are still a bit sore from the walk here
or because this sofa has a floral design that my
tattoos just so happen to match,
which naturally, makes me think of death
and to get up and leave would mean moving onto
the next thing and the thing after that
then the next thing you know we'll be back here except
on the other side of the street and I'd
actually rather stay here indefinitely,
and pretend that time doesn't exist.

DAD

This morning was greeted with
He would be so proud of you and *I wish he was here to share this with us.*
Every celebration is made bittersweet by grief.

Before mass, you asked the shop assistant to get a specific poetry collection you'd
heard about on the radio for me.

During mass, I wiped tears from your cheeks with the satin of my blouse.
My arm linked yours and my head met your shoulder.

8 years on and somehow this is where we are.
I don't know where I'd be without your open mind,
your gifted necklaces,
your spontaneous photoshoots by the gay village.

Where is dad in all of this?
He is in every photograph,
every *our father*,
every standing ovation.
He is in every belted-out hymn,
every train journey back home,
and every book of poetry.

My stress relief candle is lit next to my
yoga blocks from Amazon and
browwwwwwwwwwwwwwwwwwwn noise
brooooooooooooooown noise
yoga with Adrienne is playing on YouTube and
I didn't know Himalayan salt lamps were made of salt
I thought they just had that name just because
brooooooooooooooooooown noise
focus on the browwwwwwwwwwwwwwn noise
I still asked for one for my birthday and
books are better than films and
these are the things your mother should have taught you and
intuitive eating is the way forward and
if it's green and in a glass bottle I will
buy it for £10 per millilitre
if it has turmeric and says *detox* on it and
browwwwwwwwwwwwwn noise
brooooooooooooooooooooooooown noise
is really good for concentration
I take the day 30 minutes at a time to
get stuff done all whilst listening to
browwwwwwwwwwwwwwwwn noise
brooooooooooooooooooooown noise
and this crystal on my for you page is too powerful
it will heal me too well
so be ready for it be ready for it be ready for

.

He puts popcorn in my
mouth. I accept, kiss
his fingertips,
even though I've never
liked it sweet.

Take your top off for me,
please,
for a bit,
let me feel your skin on my skin
you feel so good,
let me squeeze
and spank
and lick
and pin
and push
you off the mattress

I jump off, rip my skin off along with his sweatshirt and
run.

SICK DOG

I am on hold,
sitting on the edge of the bed of the boy
I met last week.
Why won't the vet pick up?
It's ok, maybe there's a more sickly
animal that requires more
attention and my phone only charges at a certain
angle and I might move to the
floor instead of this bed.

The boy told me he wants to be
Hugh Grant. That we should
watch *Four Weddings and a Funeral*
and come at the same time whilst I choke
his neck. Call in sick to work and I
will cancel all my plans
and think about talking
to you with my eyes.
Hold my middle and I'll
just leave a voicemail for the vet,
begging them to call me back.

OTHER PEOPLE

are throwing up in the kitchen sink while on the phone to their ex are falling over
while trying to leapfrog
are telling the truth
are being told they should quit drinking
are having two-day hangovers
are tearing their hamstrings
are falling on their faces
are wandering off without telling their mates
are losing their phones
are spray painting FUCK TERFS on the wall
are shagging strangers on the way home
are ranking their housemates from favourite to least to their faces
are punching walls
are kissing their friends
are trying to do the worm
are thinking about their next drink when they're still on their first are kissing strangers
are passing out on doorsteps
are smoking
are throwing up until 4am in their Tinder date's bathroom post-shag
are falling asleep in the bath
are crying
are buying the entire bar
are dying
are throwing up into the Thames next to the boy they fancy
are stealing fur coats
are upsetting their boyfriends
are getting locked out of their rooms
are getting refused entry
are dancing in the middle of winter in the rain
are beefing the bouncer
are climbing towers they can't get down from
are passing out on stranger's sofas
are spitting in other people's faces
are threatening
are mistaking hand sanitiser for lube
are rubbing dicks
are running into traffic
are forgetting

are doing ket
are falling into rose bushes
are performing spells on empty pint glasses
are shouting back at the comedian on stage
are slipping down the stairs
are shagging the guy their friend really likes
are begging
are running through walls
are stealing from behind the bar
are getting in debt
are stumbling home at 15 after two pitchers of cocktails are making out with their fridge
are screaming
are saying they're from Wisconsin when actually they're Irish are becoming best friends with girls in the toilets are kissing people who don't want it
are singing kumbaya
are getting carried by binmen
are having their hair held back
are falling into Drag Queens
are climbing rooftops
are driving cars
are repeating
are hallucinating
are telling everyone to buy them a drink
are saying *I love you* too soon.

THE WAY I USE THEM MAKES ME FEEL BETTER THAN EVERYONE ELSE ONE SEC AND COMPLETELY

Worthless the next,
like if I *don't* do poetry,
I feel like shit, but if I drink
and drink
and drink
and drink
and drink I end up back with you trying to kiss me and watching fifteen years of
friendship dissipate when I refuse,
and now here I am, hungover as hell,
four years later,
in Camberwell,
bumping into the strangers we've become.

MORNING SEX

You can be the white hotel hand towel,
easily replaceable and not as hard as you think to get
the mud stains from my white trainers out in the sink.

I will try to clean up afterwards, but
I am the trainers,
so there's only so much I can do when

you move me from dirty to slightly
wet, drying out alone and a little bit
cold on the balcony.

PLEASE

Fill my cup with slippery sleep
and I will down it
in one, by which I mean I will take intermittent sips.

I want to sit
soft and live
hard. I will cushion
myself in the corner
of the room and rub
the small of your back until
it is whole, or at the very least until you are warm.

1. habits different from
2. worrying will or will not help me
3. alone no one will see
4. make uncontrollable larger
5. I make myself
6. cutting hiding chewing spitting swallowing refusing
7. with angry interest pleasure
8. I would never
9. fat.
10. panic
11. fear gaining
12. control
13. all my friends unable to
14. (females only)
15. irregular
16. dieting, exercising, fitness,
17. alone
18.

Found

WATER BOY

When I first saw water boy, he was face
up reflecting the sun
limbs submerged in splash crinkles

I knew then he was magic.
He was water boy,
not to be confused with merman
only water and limbs and boy
and the wet wash

when water made way for wet mud
wine, theatre tickets and butterfly kisses
there were no voices.

Water boy does whatever he wants
so I do whatever I want.

I take in the long overdue sun,
I take in cold on my outstretched arms
by which I mean, connection,
by which I mean, free.

HOT GIRL WALK

I see you, headphones over ears, jogging bottoms on, bra: optional.
You are praying you don't bump into anyone you know, because this time is for YOU,
This park is YOURS,
Ugly walking shoes ON,
Sweat condensing on your forehead, this is real
Hot girl shit
This
Is not for the boys so
I won't blame you if you stick your ankle out for a man to trip up on in fact,
I encourage it,
Trip them all up,
Especially when it's a group of them,
Especially when they don't move out of the way for you to walk by,
Men will not ruin the sanctity of the hot girl walk,
Oh,
Hot girl walk,
Podcast listening baddies
Your cap is ON
And Paris Hilton's memoir is playing in your ears this
Is the divine feminine
This
Is what you need in the year of our Barbie movie and
My god
The breeze
The trees
The conkers
The simplicity.

The sun is picnicking today,
Fully equipped with gingham blanket, bluetooth speaker and chocolate covered
everything dripping in ooze and schmooze and she's wooing me today.
As I lay back on the green and take her in,
my skin blushes in her radiance,
I am almost drunk on her warmth.
She is golden, pure golden,
and everything is better now she is here.

I am all citrus mornings cleanse me before my first poo bed head sleep in eyes I am lucky to be here I am lucky to be alive and if you have been touched by grief this week or at any other time know that you can put it in my hands. I know that you can't give all of it but at least give me some I will try to hold it but if I fail, if the weight of your grief is too heavy for both of us I will just hold you instead.

KARA

You are feeding me pasta as I do the dishes at the Afters.
I would never let anyone else share this moment,
to be at such mutual service as my stomach
gratefully growls.

It has been three long, full
days of oversharing, bossing
around and throwing myself
around this quiet town that didn't
know what hit it.

Until now, I've been filling
every moment with not-so-subtle
parent flirting, staying fuelled
on *I only need a coffee, it's fine.*

Doing the dishes is less an act of kindness,
and more a thinly veiled excuse to not have to
talk to anyone, whilst still feeling
useful.

You are not only feeding me,
but adding to the absence of speech by
filling my mouth up.
I almost hate
that I've made this into

a poem because it existed so
peacefully in the kitchen that
turned out to have a hidden
dishwasher all along.

FRANCIS

Outside the comedy club,
we are gripped in that first kiss tingle.

We have just seen one comedian make jokes about trans people.
Another, more famous comedian, is about to stumble on the stage,
spewing nonsense, one hand on the mic holding him up and the other on a bottle of
prosecco, a balancing act.

To both, I'm rolling my eyes,
but the ally of your elbow nudges mine, asks me if I'm alright.
you will check again, later, when the more famous comedian is negging me outside.
And sure, it helps we're already friends,
that I've always sort of fancied you,
always done the "what if" mental gymnastics with,

Some might call it the night,
I call it the dark space between our two bodies,

Some might say the night is that negging comedian,
those "you're a bit chubby but I like chubby girls" type of men,
and the violent hangover at work the next day.

But for me, the night is the nudging of elbows,
the "did you get home safely?" text,
it is us, drunk and intertwined,
and this is the night I want.

HOLBORN SPOONS

Imagine thinking that you can come over to the two girls sitting alone and drinking a pint and a glass of sparkling rosé and who, conveniently, aren't sitting with any men and who are brand new friends,

imagine coming up to them and saying
"Hahaha I would guess you're strippers, hahahah I'm only kidding, wow you're so defensive, also I'm a feminist"

and "where are you from? Like where are your parents from because I think your name sounds like labia I'm a feminist that's so hot are you on the apps? Where do you put your age range? I try my best not to pay for sex but I am divorced hahahahahahahahahah!"

And thank god a friend of a friend just so happens to be at this Holborn spoons with two boys who are kind and I know her and I both hate relying on them to cushion us in the bubble wrap of male guilt like we're made out of china or makeup and nice outfits but I'm glad because they are making us laugh.

You'd think three boys sitting around us would stop labia man from coming back, but naturally, nothing can stop the who are these guys man, the oh you have a boyfriend man, the oh you have a boyfriend so I will only focus on your friend man, the I will buy you a drink but not you because fuck you, you have a boyfriend man, the 40 year old man talking to what he thinks are two uni students man,

and I am waiting, still waiting for him to fuck off or to at least PayPal both of us to make up for this.

the same people ░ same event

we're here to celebrate

only ones I have left, ░ weird ░ *how have you been*

do you remember when we

once ░ still

lingers ░ get drunker and

and drunker

July ░ boiling ░ sometimes

prosecco'ed up in the park ░ boy if

I could have some of his beer ░ a half

fat rum ░ juice ░ wavy and

so warm ░ gender ░ asking someone

else if ░ gay

answers

the boy who ░ beer

been together for the past 4

I celebrate her birthday ░ Christmas

and ░ tells me 45k

fuck this, I want to be inside,

WHEN I SPEAK OF LOVE
After Kareem Parkins Brown

when I speak of love,
I speak of the conkers you used to keep in your blazer,
post-lesson vegan mac and cheese,
our conversations about gender and piercings
wrapped in the bisexual pride flag

I speak of swapping men in clubs
as easily as compliments in the loo,
peppering our gossip with
                      but who am I to judge?
                      maybe I'm deeping it too much, but

I speak of writing letters across oceans,
sneaking Tesco strawberry laces between the pages,
day trips taken to get heart shaped tattoos in Spain,

I speak of endless episodes of drag race and your baby,
all dimples and perfect, pinning honorary auntie status
like a badge to the lapel of my pride,

we will never Bendelacreme our way
out of each other's lives because it's All Stars 7 rules,
you, a vision of loveliness and white dress and flowers,
fixing the red of my lip and day drinking
on Clapham Common, putting the world to rights

when I speak of love,
I speak of our coated December bodies
amongst the poison bottles and post cards
and we are belting out COLLECTING YOUR
JAR OF HEARTS and
I know there is no way that any of this love will ever be torn apart,

it just can't, and maybe that's why we are giggling
when we sing, our world is barbie land on steroids,
and although our hearts have been bruised
they have never been broken, could never be broken,
not with all this love to speak of,
there is so much but never too much,
this Goldilocks just-right love.

Wanting/found

THIRST TRAP

A boy is spitting at me,
he is following me down the road and
I keep walking
I keep walking
I keep walking
and a friend of a friend of a friend is not letting
my hand go, Maria is punching another
guy in the face for touching her and
little does spit boy know, spitting is my kink so salivate on me baby it's a win-win
especially hate spit, especially anti-women spit, especially spit from a boy who
thinks I'm a woman it's so nice, it feels so good like did he know spit is 99% water,
how did he know I was thirsty, so thirsty, so insatiably thirsty

ADHD

My housemate thinks I might have ADHD.
They tell me their symptoms which sound like similes
to the way I put my shoes on at least thirty minutes before leaving the house so I
can feel ready and
my housemate thinks I might have ADHD,
when his body language matches mine it makes it easier
to cross off "drink coffee" from my to do list
and my housemate thinks I might have ADHD,
only when I'm listening to a podcast can I put away laundry,
put dinner in the oven, reply to texts about wedding gifts and
think about writing three belated cards,
before I can sit on the sofa and next to my housemate who thinks I might have
ADHD,
the sofa where our conversations refuse to follow a single thread,
but follow fidget rings and tiktok scrolls and rearranging the bookshelf and did
you see they broke up and have you eaten dinner yet? I have to tell you about what
happened earlier and I'm searching back through my emails for signs,
wondering how far they can stretch back in time until I find
I'm finally getting my diagnosis,
I've even gone so far as to fill out -

IT'S THE PERFECT EXCUSE

to not reply to texts
for a day off
for a takeaway
for anxiety
for a cuddle
for Netflix
to not exercise
to cry
to reinvent yourself
to detox
for a cleanse
for a face mask
to keep the blinds down
to stay in bed
to cancel
to not drink tonight,
because the thought of it makes you sick,
which makes you think you don't have a problem,
because if you did, you'd be right back on it,
because you don't have a problem,
but when your liver feels cleaner,
and self-pity becomes a new day.

I wish I hadn't met you when *About Time* came out
you: all red and rosy
me: wanting so badly
my fringe cut too short
slow burn blush dimpling in place pretty
girl next to you I don't know what I was apart
from sixteen recently bereaved begging
you to fill the air in the circle of my arms
Bill dies just like my dad
it's still my favourite film
sorry for the spoilers you were just ginger
could have been a tory for all I cared
Tim (in the film) probably was let's face it
white + somerset + barrister +
going back in time to stalk Rachel McAdams
what would the film have been if she was all Regina George
my fringe was so terrible I would have gone bleach blonde
blending Regina and Margot Robbie the one that got
the one who could see through red bumbling bullshit
I am so disinterested in a life without being able
to go back in time to do anything other than stalky stalk
the conversations that could be had
it's still my favourite film

ARE YOU DRINKING AGAIN

Is like asking me *are you a woman*
or do you like men yes,
sometimes, it's a love-hate thing.

ALEX

My feelings sit on my skin,
which is maybe why it feels so soft,
even without moisturiser.
I look at her over our second pint.
We were only coming for one.

She brings fingerprints to my
feelings, brailling them in *I know*.
I didn't think it was possible for my skin to get
softer, until she goes
I know what this is really about.
and now my skin is so dry,
no amount of cocoa butter can fix it.

COFFEE FOR TWO

Lately I've been making enough coffee for two and pouring away the rest
its succulent sweet bitter sweet bitter sweet caffeine fuels me before noon
no food just coffee
coursing through lanes and it takes a little while to make so I'm forced to practice
patience but I want there to be no interim between my lips and the rim of my
COFFEE PERSON mug nor my brain and my fingertips opening my home page
This morning the coffee pot has been working away
letting electricity through its veins drip feeding into heart
the fingertips of the timer tap my forehead
black blood transfused into pot and all the while I'm in the shower because
God forbid I could just wait.

The coffee is ready for me.
I eat it from the inside out.
I leave huge breaks between messages.
I don't want to freak her out.
I want to know if she takes sugar, cream,
I can't tell her straight away
how much I'd like to take her out for a coffee.

CAMBERWELL GREEN

A man is helping his wife readjust her coat before he takes her by the arm.
He doesn't need to say he loves her
for me to hear it from the other side of the park.

They are as small as
the last dregs of our first pints together,
warmed by the buzz of hormones and beer,
overlooking SE5 from the *Fox on the Hill.*

The couple have now stopped
in the middle of the Burgess Park bridge.
They take in the muggy sky and council estates
smiling across this skyline.

One day we might be them,
but for now, meet me at the Green in an hour.

We'll get wraps from the falafel shop,
find a patch of grass that isn't studded with cigarette butts and broken bottle glass,
take in the scent of cheap weed.
I will tell you that this is the Green
of first kisses,
of after-school *Morleys*,
of *i'll be home soon* texts to mums,
of interweaving the fabrics of different upbringings.

When it gets dark maybe we'll go to our first-date pub,
maybe we'll stumble out and you'll readjust my coat,
take me by the arm and walk me home.

ACKNOWLEDGEMENTS

Huge thank you to Aaron Kent and the entire Broken Sleep team, for believing in my work and for giving this pamphlet a home. I am so grateful that *Rein It In* is out with such a gorgeous press that brings so much to the publishing industry.

I owe so much gratitude to the Creative Writing tutors at the University of Birmingham. Thank you especially to Luke Kennard for all your advice and support throughout and beyond my university studies.

With special thanks to Matt Sowerby, Francis-Xavier Mukiibi, and George Ttoouli for providing in depth, caring feedback for this pamphlet and shaping it into what it is today. Thank you for always giving time for me and my poems.

Thank you to the *Everything* poetry community for holding me. I am so grateful to run this poetry night in such a vibrant and chaotic city. Thank you to all the poets and supporters of poets I have met across the London poetry scene.

Thank you to the Birmingham poetry scene, without which I would not write poetry. Special thanks to *Grizzly Pear*, which is the first regular poetry night I ever went to back in 2018. It is one of the longest running poetry nights in Birmingham and will always hold such value to me.

Thank you to every person who is in each of these poems, either explicitly or implicitly.

Huge hugs to my family for shaping who I am and for being supportive of my creativity.

Big love to all my friends, new and old, with special thanks to my best friend, Chloe Murr. Thank you for always supporting me and being so generous with your time and for holding so much space for me. You are the best!

'Please' was first published in *Life's Wonders* (Black Pear Press, 2023)

LAY OUT YOUR UNREST

Milton Keynes UK
Ingram Content Group UK Ltd.
UKHW021936150524
442683UK00004B/173

9 781916 938229